D0717737

HARTLEPOOL BOROUGH
WITHDRAWN
LIBRARIES

1690512 1

POLYMER CLAYWORK

HARTLEPOOL BOROUGH LIBRARIES

NEW CRAFTS

POLYMER CLAYWORK

25 creative projects shown step by step

MARY MAGUIRE

PHOTOGRAPHY BY STEVE DALTON

LORENZ BOOKS

This edition is published by Lorenz Books,
an imprint of Anness Publishing Ltd,
108 Great Russell Street,
London WC1B 3NA;
info@anness.com

www.lorenzbooks.com; www.annesspublishing.com;
twitter: @Anness_Books

If you like the images in this book and would like to investigate
using them for publishing, promotions or advertising, please visit
our website www.practicalpictures.com for more information.

© Anness Publishing Ltd 2015

All rights reserved. No part of this publication may be reproduced,
stored in a retrieval system, or transmitted in any way or by any
means, electronic, mechanical, photocopying, recording or otherwise,
without the prior written permission of the copyright holder.

A CIP catalogue record for this book
is available from the British Library.

Publisher: Joanna Lorenz
Photographer: Steve Dalton
Stylist: Sue Pitman
Illustrators: Vana Haggerty and Madeleine David
Designer: Lucy Doncaster
Production Controller: Rosanna Anness

PUBLISHER'S NOTE
Although the advice and information in this book are believed
to be accurate and true at the time of going to press, neither the
authors nor the publisher can accept any legal responsibility or
liability for any errors or omissions that may have been made nor
for any inaccuracies nor for any loss, harm or injury that comes
about from following instructions or advice in this book.

ACKNOWLEDGEMENTS
The author and publisher wish to thank the following for
contributing projects to this book: Julia Hill – Picture Frame
(page 72); Anne Dyson – Mirror with Lizards (page 49); Dawn
Emms – Glow-in-the-Dark Clock (page 68); Sandra Duvall – Tiger
Door Plaque (page 40); Kitchen Table Studios – Egyptian Bangle
(page 62), Starburst Hand Mirror (page 88), Ornamental Book
Cover (page 91); Theresa Pateman – Three-dimensional Picture
(page 36), Mobile Jugglers (page 43); Rebecca Patterson – Poly
Mermaid (page 46); Helen Mahoney for the knitted toys with
the Tiny Tea Set (page 82).

    Thanks also to the following for supplying materials for this book:
Alec Tiranti, Green & Stone, Cornelisson & Son, and V V Rouleaux.

CONTENTS

INTRODUCTION

Polymer clay is a versatile, easy to handle modelling medium that can be used for making objects as diverse as jewellery, miniature tea sets, dolls, toy theatres, lamps, tableware and mirror surrounds. Known to doll and model makers for decades, this material is now widely available for anyone to use and new techniques are being developed all the time.

Similar in some ways to ordinary clay, polymer clay has many advantages. It is made in a wide range of colours, including some with glow-in-the dark properties, and colours can be mixed or juxtaposed to create intricate effects. It does not shrink, making it suitable for embedding objects, and once baked it is waterproof and durable. In addition, it can be treated with metallic finishes.

All you need to work with polymer clay are your hands, a knife, a table and a domestic oven, although specialized tools will be necessary for more advanced techniques. The skills required are easy to learn, and once you have acquired them and made some of the more advanced projects, you will be able to embark on your own designs.

Left: Polymer clay can be used to create a dazzling array of objects, from simple buttons to jolly cutlery and eye-catching decorations for the home.

HISTORY OF POLYMER CLAY

Polymer clay originated in Germany in the late 1930s. It was an accidental chemical by-product that was discovered by Mrs Rehbinder, the daughter of the famous doll-maker Käthe Kruse. During the Second World War she did not have a suitable raw material to make dolls' heads from. She experimented with this by-product and found that it could be modelled and hardened in an oven. She continued to experiment with the material for some years, using it to create mosaics, as well as for her initial purpose of dolls' heads. She developed a limited colour range, which she started to sell under the name of Fifi Mosaik – derived from her nickname Fifi and its mosaic application.

Until 1964 Mrs Rehbinder marketed her product alone, without advertising. Then she approached Eberhard Faber and acquired a licence for industrial production. The product is now bought as Fimo.

Sculpey, the American equivalent, was developed in the late 1960s by a company called Polyform products in Illinois. Other brands of polymer clay include Formello, Modello, Cernit, Promat, Kato Polyclay and Pardo. The quality of polymer clay has improved greatly since it first came on to the market. Each brand has its own colour range, and they all differ in consistency and cooking directions, so it is important to read the instructions.

Because its history is fairly recent, the medium is still establishing and defining itself – and polymer clay artists tend to draw heavily on well-established methods from other disciplines. The most popular of these are cane work and millefiori, techniques that are now undergoing something of a renaissance.

Below: An example of the late medieval art of millefiori: a glass bead embellished with canes and traces of gilding.

Above: Cane work was used in Ancient Egypt to produce faces made from mosaic glass slices. The two slices here show an exaggerated expression on a male face, suggestive of a Greek mask.

These partner arts of glassworking are thought to have developed in Mesopotamia and quality works of great craftsmanship were being produced in Alexandria and ancient Egypt. The art was rediscovered by the Italians in the late 15th century. It was they who called it millefiori, which literally means 'a thousand flowers'.

Cane work is used to make a batch of multiple images. Long coloured rods of glass are placed next to each other to form a picture or pattern and fused together so that the picture runs through the length of the cane (most people will be familiar with this technique as applied to the confection seaside rock). Slices are taken from the cane at this point, or the picture or pattern can be miniaturized by a process called reduction – by rolling the molten canes they can be elongated, then sliced. These little miniatures can be applied to the surface of a glass bead, under a hot flame. This process is known as lampwerk. The slices are fused side by side on to the surface of the bead, until the bead is completely covered – hence millefiori.

This is an enchanting technique with various applications, many of which are very popular. Elaborate beads and paperweights made by Murona craftsmen, or those from the French company Campagne des Cristallenes de Baccavat, are much sought after by collectors.

Polymer clay is ideally suited to this ancient technique, and brings new dimensions to the art form. What the medium lacks in transparency it makes up for in its versatility, attracting collectors in its own right.

Above: Cane work and millefiori, ancient techniques in the art of glasswork, have proved to be extremely well suited to the modern material, polymer clay.

Left: In cane work, long rods of pictures are made, from which slices are taken. For the further stage of millefiori, above, the slices of cane are then used to completely cover a plain bead, providing diverse, intricate decoration. (Beads and picture canes by Ingrid Proudfoot.)

GALLERY

There is no doubt about the huge potential of polymer clay as an art medium, and exciting and innovative developments are occurring all the time. A growing number of artists have recognized the unique properties of polymer clay and used them to develop their own particular styles and techniques. To inspire you to explore and experiment with this fascinating material, this gallery section includes examples of artists' work which help to show the material's versatility and attraction.

Left: CITY ZEN CANE David Forlano and Steven Ford trained as painters at the Tyler School of Art in Rome, where they drew inspiration for their mosaic picture frames and eggs. Each design consists of thousands of tiny coloured squares of various tints to make them look like ancient stone. The eggs are made by placing cane slices of real shells from blown-out duck and goose eggs. Founding members of the National Polymer Guild in the USA, both artists teach intermediate and advanced polymer clay workshops.

Below: HEART BROOCH AND FLOWER JEWELLERY Lara Bohnic designs jewellery and also works as a product and fashion designer. Attracted by the lightness, colour and easy workability of one of the softer polymer clays, she takes her inspiration from nature, pop art and kitsch culture.

Left: PEOPLE BEADS
These people beads were made by Cynthia Troop by layering tiny pieces of polymer clay on to a basic bead, then incorporating cane work into the costumes. Each bead was unique and could take anything from several hours to a few weeks to complete.

Below: PAPERWEIGHTS Ingrid Proudfoot began experimenting with making polymer clay jewellery in the 1980s, and has gone on to make a wide variety of artefacts, including buttons, door knobs, clocks and umbrella handles. She mainly uses cane work in which a strong African influence is detectable.

Below: IRIDESCENT EARRINGS
Mary Maguire has been making polymer clay jewellery since 1986. She prefers to use just one base colour with a metal leaf applied to the surface, and likes to incorporate shells and other found objects into her work.

Right: MINIATURE THEATRE
Theresa Pateman first used polymer clay to make jewellery, but when she discovered its versatility she began creating figures around wire armature. Inspired by a visit to the Musée Grevin in Paris, she devised this miniature theatre.

Right: BROOCHES
These two brooches (pins) were made by Lindly Haunani using a technique adapted from the Japanese metalworking art of Mokume Gane, which usually consists of laminating thin sheets of silver, gold and copper alloy, fusing the layers together, then distorting the shape to create a watermark or woodgrain pattern when sliced through. This effect is much easier to achieve with polymer clay by layering thin slices of translucent clay, which have very small amounts of colour mixed in, and silver leaf. The block is then deformed to create an uneven surface and thin slices are taken off it. These are then collaged on to the surface of a base shape.

Right: HAT PIN AND JEWELLERY *Sandra Duvall and Julia Hill designed this hat pin, three-piece brooch and brooch-and-earring set, which are all made by the millefiori* technique. *They also specialize in buttons, hairslides (barrettes), drop earrings, cufflinks and tie pins, drawing their inspiration from Matisse and primitive decoration.*

Below: CLOCK JEWELLERY *Having previously made jewellery for a decade, Eileen Mahony began using polymer clay in about 1990. Her soft watches are built up from three-dimensional layers of* clay, then gilded with bronze powders and the numerals painted on, influenced by Dali's painting The Persistence of Memory. *She also makes psychedelic millefiori jewellery, as well as small boxes and mirrors.*

Left: GILDED
BROOCHES
*Drawing from their
backgrounds in
illustration and
ceramics, Eric Pateman
and Fiona French (of
Kitchen Table Studio)
taught themselves the
art of jewellery making.
They lay gold and
silver leaf on to polymer
clay, then paint the
cooked pieces. Their
work has strong Celtic
and Egyptian flavours.*

Left: BLACK AND GOLD
CANDLESTICKS
*Sarah Nelson Shriver makes
jewellery and decorations
out of polymer clay. These
candlesticks are 25cm (10in)
high, with an interior vertical
support of nylon-reinforced
plastic tubing. The decorative
elements were applied using
the millefiori technique.*

Below: FACE PINS
*Iridian Faces are vibrant
character face pins that were
created by Ellen Watt. She has
been making the faces since
1989, and each one is unique.
Ellen uses customized cookie
cutters to form the basic
shapes from polymer clay
slabs. They are hand-
manipulated from there
to form characterful pieces.*

Left: HEARTS
OF GOLD
*Deborah Banyas and
T. P. Speer are sculptors
working with polymer
clay. This piece was
constructed out of wood
and stuffed cotton. The
polymer clay was then
applied, and the piece
finished in acrylic
paint and gold leaf.*

MATERIALS

Polymer clay is actually a plastic known as polyvinyl chloride. It is clean to work with, it does not shrink and it is already coloured, making glazing or painting unnecessary except for creating effects. Baking polymer clay in an ordinary domestic oven at 102–135°C (215–275°F), according to the manufacturer's instructions, fuses particles together in the polymerization process, transforming the clay from a malleable substance into a solid one. Once baked, the clay can be sanded, sawn, drilled and glued. Various brands of polymer clay are sold. Although they are all basically the same, some have a slightly different consistency, and some are more specifically designed as economical modelling clay for making dolls and models. Experience will soon tell you which ones you prefer for different types of project. There is an ever-increasing range of colours available, including fluorescent, pearlescent and metallic colours, as well as glow-in-the-dark, transparent and mottled stone effects. Most manufacturers sell their clays in small blocks that weigh about 65g (2oz), but for economy, larger blocks are available in limited colour ranges, as well as the specialized modelling clay.

Doll-making polymer clay is stiffer than most and is available in large blocks.

Modelling polymer clay is easier to work but stronger once baked, and is available in large blocks.

Pearlescent polymer clay has a creamy, attractive sheen.

Translucent polymer clay can be used in a number of interesting ways.

Glow-in-the-dark polymer clay can be used for items that usefully show up in the dark.

Mix quick polymer clay is soon workable and suitable for use by children.

Mottled stone An imitation stone effect can be applied to polymer clay in a number of colours.

Glamour colours provide a metallic effect on polymer clay.

Softer polymer clay is available in a range of colours.

Fluorescent and ordinary colours are exciting and fun to use.

Epoxy resin glue Used in two parts, this is very stong glue.

Aluminium wire can be used for building support structures.

Jewellery wire is used for connecting pieces for earrings and necklaces.

Metallic leaf in gold, silver, copper and aluminium is used for decorating the surface of clay.

Fridge magnets are produced by polymer clay manufacturers for use with their clays.

Button backs are useful for making polymer clay buttons.

Slide base (baronette) Useful for fixing the finished item to something else.

Beads and gemstones These must be flat-backed and, if they are to go into the oven, made of glass.

Clip-on earring backs and metal button backs are used to make jewellery pieces.

Bronze powders A limited range is produced by polymer clay manufacturers.

Varnish, gloss or matt (flat), is supplied by polymer clay manufacturers.

Acrylic paint can be used for covering the surface of polymer clay.

Enamel paint is used for painting small areas or patterns.

Key
1 Doll-making polymer clay
2 Modelling polymer clay
3 Dilutant
4 Pearlescent polymer clay
5 Translucent polymer clay
6 Glow-in-the-dark polymer clay

7 Mix quick polymer clay
8 Mottled stone effect
9 Glamour colours
10 Softer polymer clay
11 Fluorescent and ordinary colours
12 Epoxy resin glue
13 Aluminium wire
14 Jewellery wire
15 Metallic leaf
16 Fridge magnets
17 Button back
18 Slide base (baronette)
19 Beads and gemstones
20 Clip-on earring backs and metal button backs
21 Bronze powders (branded)
22 Bronze powders
23 Acrylic paint
24 Enamel paint

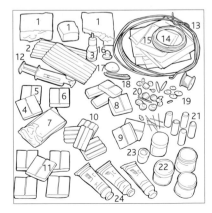

EQUIPMENT

In addition to an ordinary household oven, the most important tools required for working with polymer clay are your hands. When you first start, household items gleaned from kitchen drawers and sewing, knitting and tool boxes will do. Dressmaking pins, knitting needles, cheese cutters, screws, pens and even matchsticks can all be improvised as tools, and you will find that a variety of objects can produce patterns. But for more advanced work, some specialized equipment will be useful. Whatever equipment you use for polymer clay, keep it exclusively for that purpose and never use it for preparing food.

Oven An oven is necessary for baking the clay at a specified temperature. If you prefer not to place plastic materials in their domestic ovens, at least one polymer clay manufacturer markets a special oven.

Mirror Placed behind the work, a mirror will enable you to see all around when slicing large canes or blocks, ensuring neat, even cuts.

Oven thermometer Using an oven thermometer ensures that your oven is working at the correct temperatures for the clay. This is important because undercooked clay can be fragile and overcooking burns the clay.

Pasta machine This can be used for rolling out clay to different thicknesses and is helpful when precision and evenness are required, especially when producing several sheets of the same thickness. It can also be used for mixing colours. Buy one just for use with polymer clay and do not wash it between different colours – just wipe it clean with a cloth.

Dust mask Always wear a dust mask when sanding or drilling baked polymer or when using bronze powders.

Aluminium foil Layers of foil can be used to create bulk when making up shapes.

Greaseproof (waxed) paper Tape a sheet of greaseproof paper to your work surface to ensure a smooth area. Also useful for placing clay on when baking.

Punches Metal- and leather-working punches are good for indenting and texturing clay surfaces.

Dentistry tools These precision tools are excellent for modelling. Ask your dentist for old ones or you can buy them from modelling stores.

Pastry cutter Good for patterns or cutting zigzag edges.

Dividers Useful for marking out circular shapes to be cut out.

Cocktail sticks (toothpicks) Good for reinforcing structures, especially joints.

Straws These can be used for making holes big enough for ribbon to pass through or for hanging over a nail.

Kebab sticks Use these to hold beads during baking.

Scissors are an essential piece of equipment useful for cutting out card or paper templates.

Cheese slice This can be used for taking even slices from an oblong cane.

Soft dough cutters For cutting out a wide variety of shapes, dough cutters are useful but you may have to trim the edges of plastic ones to make them sharper.

Airtight sandwich box Uncooked polymer clay has a shelf life of about 2 years but goes crumbly if exposed to heat and ultraviolet light. Wrap the raw clay in greaseproof paper before storing it in a box.

Craft (utility) knife and scalpel A craft knife is good for cutting out cardboard while a scalpel is perhaps the most useful tool for working with polymer clay.

Plastic cutting mat To protect your work surface always cut clay on a cutting mat.

Scrub the mat thoroughly to remove all trace of clay after use, as residues seem to react with the mat material.

Tissue blade Designed for taking human tissue samples, these razor-sharp blades enable thin slices to be cut from clay, and they are especially useful in canework.

Round-nosed (snub-nosed) jeweller's pliers Use these when making up polymer jewellery pieces.

Pliers are essential for bending wire used structurally in projects.

Wire cutters are for cutting wire.

Vinyl gloves Many people prefer to wear gloves to protect their hands. Others wear them so as not to leave fingerprints on the clay. Gloves should be changed with each change of colour to avoid transferring residual polymer particles from one colour to another.

Fine palette knife or spatula This is useful for lifting thinly rolled-out polymer clay.

Paintbrushes are essential for applying bronze powders and paints.

Plate A plate is useful as a surface on which you can mix paint colours.

Steel ruler A steel ruler is best when cutting a straight edge with a sharp knife.

Rolling pin A vinyl or straight-sided glass roller is best for rolling out clay by hand although marble is excellent during hot weather, especially if the clay is overworked.

Brayer Sometimes referred to as a small roller, this is a good implement for smoothing over clay, used over paper, or for applying metal leaf.

Plexiglass rollers This is a home-made device consisting of a small sheet of plexiglass with a glued-on wooden block as a handle, and it is excellent for rolling out logs and canes. It is a good idea to make two sizes, about 8 x 8cm (3 x 3in) and 20 x 18cm (8in x 7in), for rolling out larger or smaller items.

Petit four and aspic cutters are handy for cutting out interesting shapes from thinly rolled polymer clay.

Clay extruder This tool is a bit difficult to use but it is helpful if you do a lot of polymer clay work. The device should be secured with a small vice and the clay must be soft or thinned before it is used.

Smoothing tools These rubber-tipped craft implements are used for smoothing areas smaller than your fingertips, and they resemble paintbrushes.

Key
1 Oven
2 Mirror
3 Oven thermometer
4 Pasta machine
5 Dust mask
6 Aluminium foil
7 Greaseproof (waxed) paper
8 Punches
9 Dentistry tools
10 Pastry cutter
11 Dividers
12 Cocktail sticks (toothpicks)
13 Straws
14 Kebab sticks
15 Scissors
16 Cheese slice
17 Soft dough cutters
18 Airtight sandwich box
19 Craft (utility) knife and scalpel
20 Plastic cutting mat
21 Tissue blade
22 Round-nosed (snub-nosed) jeweller's pliers
23 Pliers
24 Wire cutters
25 Vinyl gloves
26 Fine palette knife or spatula
27 Paintbrushes
28 Plate
29 Steel rulers
30 Rolling pin
31 Brayer
32 Plexiglass rollers
33 Petit four and aspic cutters
34 Clay extruder
35 Smoothing tools

BASIC TECHNIQUES

Polymer clay is a wonderfully versatile material, which can be shaped, moulded and modelled in various ways to produce quite different effects. Instructions are given here for the general techniques that have been applied to many of the projects in this book, so do read through this section carefully before embarking on a project. As polymer clays will pick up any dirt and dust around, it is important to make sure your hands are scrupulously clean. You will also need to wash your hands when changing from one colour to another as any residues will discolour the next piece of clay you knead.

PREPARING POLYMER CLAY

Polymer clays need to be manipulated or kneaded before they can be worked, the degree varying according to the brand. As clays are responsive to temperature, the warmth of your hands contributes to the conditioning process, and there is a world of difference between working with clay on a cold winter's day and on a hot summer's day. Some people go so far as to carry the clay in their pockets, or even next to their skin, before working it.

To get your clay to its optimal working consistency, work small amounts, about an eighth of a block at a time, in your hands. Roll it between your palms to form a sausage, bend it over and roll again, then repeat the whole process until the clay is soft and pliable. Try to avoid trapping air bubbles in the clay. A pasta-making machine can be pressed into service to help the softening process – but once you have used it for preparing polymer clay, do not use it with food.

MIXING COLOURS

Although there are several commercially available colours, the choice becomes unlimited when you mix colours yourself. You can experiment by using small amounts to tailor colours to your needs. When mixing dark and light colours, add tiny bits of the darker clay to the lighter colour as the darker one can easily overpower the lighter one.

Mixing with a Pasta-making Machine

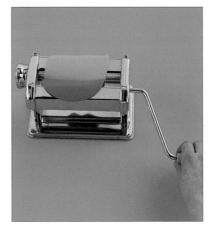

1 A pasta-making machine is excellent for mixing colours. Feed two differently coloured sheets through the machine together, feeding them from opposite sides. As they go through the machine they will become fused and any air bubbles will be squeezed out.

Mixing by Hand

1 Twist together two or more differently coloured sausages. This attractive stage is called candy cane and can be used as such.

2 Roll the cane into a smooth log then twist, stretch and double over, excluding any air bubbles, to achieve a marbled pattern. This is another stage that can be used as it is. To blend the colours fully, continue to work the clay as described.

Rolling Out

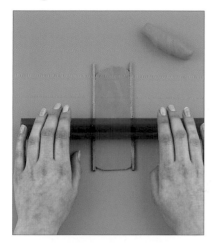

Roll out the clay on a smooth, clean surface, using a marble or acrylic rolling pin. A marble surface is excellent in a hot environment or if the clay is very soft, but is not advisable in cold conditions. To ensure an even thickness, roll the clay between two pieces of metal, wood or plastic of the depth you require, as shown in the picture above. Alternatively, pass the clay through a pasta-making machine, which is useful for producing several sheets of uniform thickness. If the clay is sticky, dust it with a thin film of flour or talcum powder.

Patterning

Patterned blocks can be used for various decorative effects. For instance, the slices of the striped block are used in the Eye-catching Cutlery project and to represent fabric in the Magnetic Theatre project, while slices of the chequerboard design are used to make the hat of one of the players in the Magnetic Theatre project. Slices can be cut off the block with a tissue blade or, if the block is long, with a cheese slice.

Striped Block

1 Roll out several sheets of differently coloured clay, trim them to the same dimensions and stack them on top of each other, smoothing each layer to exclude air bubbles. Make the last layer a different colour to the first. Trim the edges to neaten if necessary.

2 When you have stacked a few layers, cut the block in half crossways and stack. Roll with gentle pressure using a brayer.

Chequerboard Block

1 Make up a striped block. Using a tissue blade, cut off a slice the same thickness as the stripes. Stand this up alongside the block, staggering the colours, and cut another slice. Press this against the first slice and repeat to create a chequerboard block. Placing a mirror behind the block will help you ensure you slice evenly.

2 Press each side evenly against a flat surface to consolidate it. Trim if necessary.

Polka Dots

1 Press the head of a glass-headed pin into a rolled-out sheet of clay to make a regular pattern of indentations.

2 Roll out a thin sausage or cane in a contrasting colour and slice off small discs using a scalpel. Roll these into balls and press each one into an indent.

3 Place a smooth piece of paper over the clay sheet and roll it using a brayer or pass it through a pasta-making machine to smooth the surface.

Jelly Roll

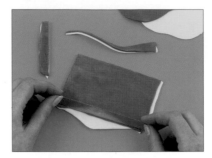

1 To make a jelly roll, roll out two or three differently coloured sheets and stack them. Trim to neaten the edges into a rectangle.

2 Roll over one of the shorter edges with a brayer to taper it.

3 Starting at the flattened end, roll up the layers tightly and evenly. Gently roll the finished cane on the flat surface, taking care not to apply too much pressure, to smooth over the seams. Trim each end flat.

Making Beads

Beads can be made in all sorts of shapes and sizes. A simple round bead is made by rolling a small ball of clay between the palms of your hands. Flat round ones are made by cutting thick discs from a log. More complicated beads can be made following the technique described in the Composite Beads project. Making the hole through the middle can be tricky as the bead has to be held firmly enough to take pressure without the shape distorting. For this reason, many people prefer to drill the hole after the clay has been baked. Make the hole large enough to take whatever the bead is to be threaded on.

1 Make a hole through an unbaked bead using a tapered point such as a thin modelling tool or darning needle, with a drilling action. When the point emerges from the other side, remove the tool and push it through from the other side to neaten the hole. After the bead has been baked, you may need to sand down around the hole gently, using abrasive paper, so that there are no jagged edges which could snag or catch on hair or clothing.

2 Beads need to be supported during baking to avoid their shapes distorting under their own weight. String the beads on wooden skewers or wire, depending on the size of their holes, and suspend them across a baking tray; make a wire support that fits in the baking tray if you make beads regularly. If you are drilling the holes after baking, place them in the folds of concertinaed card to bake them.

Cane Work

Deriving from ancient glassworking techniques, a cane is a log with a design running along its length, like a stick of rock. The designs can be simple or complex patterns or images. Thick slices cut from these canes can be made into beads or pendants. Thin slices can be used like a veneer to decorate beads or sheets of clay. Slices are best cut using a tissue blade. If necessary chill the cane before slicing to avoid distorting the shape of the soft clay.

Canes can be reduced in diameter to make delicately small designs that may also be joined together to make complex designs such as millefiori beads.

The simple flower cane shown here is used in the Night Light and the Magnetic Theatre projects. There is sufficient cane for both projects, plus enough left over for making into beads.

Simple Flower Cane

1 Roll one cane for the flower centre (yellow), two canes of another colour (green) and five canes from a third colour (pink) for the petals. Make all the canes 2cm (¾in) in diameter and 8cm (3in) long.

2 Roll out two thin sheets in different colours (coral and red) to cover the flower centre, and a large thin sheet in a colour to contrast with the petals (purple). Wrap the canes in these sheets, rolling each slightly to smooth the joins.

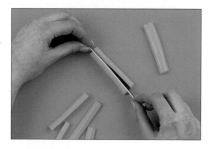

3 Using a tissue blade, cut the green canes lengthways into quarters.

4 Roll out a thin sheet of an entirely different colour (blue). Arrange the canes to form a flower, filling in the spaces between the petals with five of the quarter canes.

5 Wrap the bundle in the prepared sheet, rolling lightly to smooth the join.

6 Using a small sheet of plexiglass, roll the cane to compact it. The ends will become concave. Trim these off.

Simple Picture Cane

1 Roll a cane of white polymer clay about 3.5cm (1½in) in diameter and 8cm (3in) long. Using a tissue blade, cut it in half lengthways then cut one of the halves into two to make two quarters.

2 Roll one of the quarters into a round cane and cut it in half lengthways. Press a groove down the middle of one flat side with a thin, round wooden or metal skewer and run a thin sausage of blue clay along it. Groove the other half and sandwich the halves together to make the head and eye. Roll lightly to smooth the joins.

3 Curve the remaining half of the original white cane to form the duck's body. Place the head on the body. Cut a triangular wedge from a 1cm (½in)-diameter yellow cane 8cm (3in) long and press it against the head for the bill.

4 Pack the gaps around the duck with wedges of pale blue cane, rolled to the same length, to make a circular shape. Wrap this with a thin sheet of pale blue to hold it together and roll to consolidate it.

5 Surround the new cane with a sheet of dark blue and roll again, smoothing the join. Trim off the concave ends.

Reducing Canes

1 Roll a cane under a small sheet of plexiglass to elongate it and reduce its diameter. Trim off the resultant concave ends as you work.

2 To make canes with different diameters with the same design running through them, stop rolling at each desired size and cut the cane in half. Continue rolling one half while reserving the other. Repeat this process until you have the sizes of cane you require.

Complex Canes

Gently squeeze together several previously reduced picture or flower canes and roll them together to produce a fascinatingly complex cane.

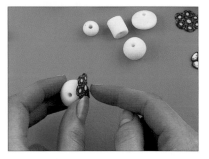

To make millefiori beads, cut thin slices from complex canes and press them on to the surface of clay beads. Previously baked beads give a better overall shape, but the millefiori slices may not adhere as well to these as they would to unbaked ones. Cover the bead completely with the thin slices and roll it between your palms to help the slices adhere.

Metallic Finishes

Polymer clays can be finished with metallic powders or metal leaf. Metal leaf may be gold, silver, copper or aluminium and is available in book form from art supply outlets. The sheets are very thin and easily marked by fingerprints so need careful handling.

Metallic powders are brushed on to the surface of the clay. They go a long way, so use them sparingly. For permanence they should be varnished. As the particles of these powders are minute and spread everywhere, a fine dust mask should always be worn when using them.

Using Metal Leaf

1 Carefully lay a sheet of transfer leaf over a sheet of rolled-out polymer clay with the metal face down. As you lay it down, roll over it using a brayer to eliminate air bubbles. Rub all over the backing tissue paper before gently and slowly peeling it off. If any metal leaf clings to the tissue paper, replace it and rub over the area with your finger.

2 If you want a cracked finish, cover the surface of the applied metal leaf with a smooth piece of paper or tissue and roll over it using a brayer until the required amount of cracking is achieved. The cracking on silver and gold is finer than on copper or aluminium.

Embossing and Texturing

Being soft and pliable, polymer clay is easy to texture. It will take the impression of any pattern you press on to its surface, such as a piece of lace, a shell or a button. Alternatively, a pattern can be sculpted on using modelling tools or leather- and metal-workers' chasing and punching tools. Textured clay can be used to make moulds for embossing other pieces of clay with a design.

1 Make a mould, such as the cup-shaped one shown here for making buttons, and transfer a relief design to it by pressing it into the clay. Bake the mould following the manufacturer's instructions, then use it to make positive images on other pieces of raw clay.

2 To highlight a textured piece before embossing, lightly brush the mould with metallic powder.

SPANGLY STARS

Stars are a perennially popular motif that is well suited to lighting. Lots of them can be quickly stamped out from a sheet of polymer clay to which gold leaf has been applied. Alternatively, paint the stars with gold paint after they have been stamped out. If you make a hole in one point of the stars, they can be dangled from the edge of the shade. You could also make lots of stars from glow-in-the-dark polymer clay and fix them to a child's bedroom ceiling.

1 Apply gold leaf to rolled-out yellow clay. Using small pastry or aspic cutters, stamp out the stars. Make some of the large ones hollow by stamping out their centres with a tiny cutter.

2 To make fixing holes, pierce the centre of the small stars and a point of the large ones using one of the jewellery head pins. If you wish, indent the centres of the small stars with a pen top for decoration.

3 Lay the stars flat on greaseproof (waxed) paper and bake them according to the manufacturer's instructions. When cool, apply varnish to protect the gold leaf.

4 Fix the stars to the lampshade using double-sided tape or jewellery head pins pushed through the holes and the shade. Twist the wires behind the shade to hold the stars in position.

Materials and Equipment You Will Need
Small block yellow polymer clay • Dutch gold leaf • Star-shaped pastry or aspic cutters • Jewellery head pins • Lampshade •
Strong doubled-sided tape • Round-nosed (snub-nosed) jeweller's pliers • Varnish • Paintbrush

JAZZY TASSELS

Tassels are expensive to buy and are usually made in an old-fashioned style, but these black-striped, fluorescent versions, which make use of inexpensive silky tassels, are fresh and lively. The polymer clay beads are modelled around a cork wrapped in aluminium foil that is removed after baking to create a hollow head through which the tassel end is threaded. Make pairs of tassels for tie-backs on curtains or single ones as light pulls.

1 Fix a marble on top of a cork or similarly shaped object using non-hardening modelling clay. Wrap a doubled strip of aluminium foil around the cork and secure with masking tape. Pinch the foil together at the top of the shape.

2 Roll out some modelling clay and cut a strip to wrap around the cork with enough to be pinched in at the top.

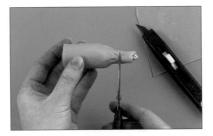

3 Snip off the excess clay at the top and smooth over to round the tassel top's shape. Push a sharp implement through the foil from the top to ensure the hole will be big enough for the tassel string. Bake for 5 minutes.

4 Pass a sharp implement through the hole at the top to push the cork out through the bottom. Roll out a thin sheet of fluorescent pink clay and wrap it around the tassel top. Cut off the excess and smooth over the join.

5 Roll or extrude thin threads of black clay. Drape these over the top of the pink clay, tucking the ends inside at the bottom. Cut off the excess.

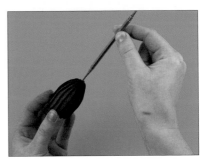

6 Press down where the threads cross over the top. Pierce through the hole once again. Return to the oven and bake for another 10 minutes. Thread the tassel through the top.

Materials and Equipment You Will Need

Marble • Cork or similar shape • Non-hardening modelling clay • Aluminium foil • Scissors • Masking tape • ⅛ block modelling polymer clay • Sharp implement such as crochet hook • Craft (utility) knife • ½ block fluorescent pink polymer clay • Small amount black polymer clay • Extruder • Tassel

BRIGHT BUTTONS

Finding just the right buttons can sometimes be tricky, especially if you want them for a garment of your own creation. With polymer clay you can make buttons to your own design and be as flamboyant as you like. At their simplest, polymer clay buttons can have two holes pricked through them for the sewing thread. Alternatively, they can be glued on to button backs; the ones used in this project are intended to be covered with fabric but polymer clay can be pressed on to them instead.

1 Snap together the two parts of each button back. Roll out coloured clay to cover the front of the button and tuck the edges into the groove at the back.

2 Make a five-petalled flower template out of card and cut one flower per button from white clay.

3 Place a flower on each clay-covered button, cover with a piece of paper and smooth over with your finger to make a good bond.

4 Make small balls in colours that contrast with the flowers, squash them into discs and press them firmly in place as flower centres. Smooth away any fingerprints.

Materials and Equipment You Will Need
Metal button backs • 1 block white polymer clay • Small amounts polymer clay: purple, turquoise, fluorescent green, yellow and pink • Thin card (stock) • Scalpel • Smooth paper

SPOTTY EGG CUPS

Covering metal objects with polymer clay is a shortcut to creating a shape, leaving only the decoration to be applied. The metal must not be previously painted or varnished. Stainless steel egg cups have been used here, but pepper and salt pots could also be treated (after removing the plastic stoppers), as could tin boxes, whistles or cutlery. A thin layer of polymer clay applied over a metal base requires just 10 minutes baking time; leave the object in the oven for a while after turning it off, to cool down.

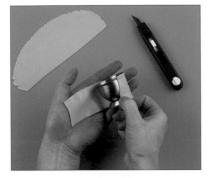

1 Roll out a thin sheet of yellow clay and cut out a strip to wrap around an egg cup.

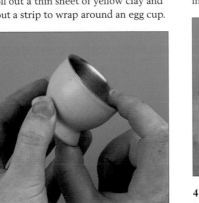

2 Smooth the clay to fit the contours of the egg cup and to join the ends together. Trim off any excess.

3 Using the beaded head of a dressmaker's pin, make small indentations in the clay in a regular pattern.

4 Roll a thin sausage of red clay. Cut this into thin slices and roll each piece into a tiny ball. Pick each one up with the sharp end of the pin and place it on an indentation in the yellow clay.

5 Use the beaded head of the pin to push the balls in position, flattening them.

6 Roll a slightly thicker red sausage to wrap around the rim, waist and bottom. Overlap the ends, trimming diagonally to fit, and smooth joins with a smoothing tool. Bake at a lower temperature, for a shorter time than recommended by the manufacturer.

Materials and Equipment You Will Need
1 block yellow polymer clay • 4 metal egg cups • Glass-headed dressmaker's pin • 1 block red polymer clay • Craft (utility) knife • Smoothing tool

CHEERY NIGHT LIGHT

The stained glass effect of this night light or candle holder gives out a warm glow while protecting the flame. A variation on traditional millefiori work, thin slices of flower cane are rolled out and used to laminate a glass tumbler. The same technique can be used to decorate glass jars, panes of glass or even goldfish bowls. When polymer clay is used this thinly, the baking time should be reduced; it is possible to bake it with a hairdryer if you can ascertain the temperature.

1 Cut five slices from the flower cane, all the same thickness (see Basic Techniques).

2 Place a piece of smooth paper over one of the slices and roll the brayer over it in different directions to thin out the flower design with minimal distortion. Check regularly that the edges are not splitting. Roll the other slices.

3 Run the brayer up and down the extra centre cane to shape it into a triangular log. Cut off 10 slices and roll them out thinly as described in step 2.

4 Make a striped block and shave off two strips using the cheese slice. Roll these between paper until they gain about 2.5cm (1in) in length.

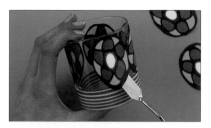

5 Wrap the thin striped slices around the bottom of the tumblers. Cut off any extra and smooth the joins. Using the palette knife or spatula, carefully transfer the flowers to the sides of the tumbler.

6 Fill the gaps between the flowers with the triangular slices. Edge the top with a thin strip of blue clay. Place the tumbler on its side and roll firmly over a hard surface. Place in the oven before it heats up and bake, reducing the recommended cooking time by 5 minutes. Allow to cool completely before removing.

Materials and Equipment You Will Need
6cm (2½in) flower cane plus centre cane (see Basic Techniques) • Craft (utility) knife • Smooth paper • Brayer • 2.5 x 10cm (1 x 4in) striped block of polymer clay: fluorescent yellow and orange (see Basic Techniques) • Cheese slice • Glass tumbler • Palette knife or spatula • Small strip blue polymer clay

THREE-DIMENSIONAL PICTURE

This enchanting picture enshrines the mythical unicorn in a theatrical setting. It can be hung on a wall by a ribbon or stood up on a shelf. The framework is made from collaged and painted cardboard while the unicorn itself is very simply modelled out of polymer clay. To enlarge the template for this and other projects, draw a grid of 2.5cm (1in) squares around the template. Draw a separate grid of larger squares and copy the template on to it.

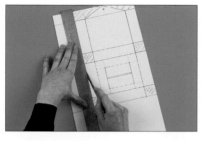

1 Draw the theatre plan on cardboard and cut out, scoring along the dotted lines (see the template at the back of the book). Make a hole where shown for hanging.

2 Using gouache paint, paint the theatre surround outside purple, the stage yellow and the ceiling blue with yellow stars. When the paint is dry, paint the backdrop blue with yellow stars. Stick a photograph of a pair of velvet curtains to the front. When dry, varnish the front for protection.

3 Glue the wings to the front of the stage at all points of contact. Fold along all the score lines. Glue the top backdrop to the edges of the wings.

4 Fold the sides in and glue along the edges and fix to the back.

5 Shape the unicorn form. Pinch out the head, legs and tail shape, using a modelling tool for detail if you wish. Bake following the manufacturer's instructions. When the model is cool, smooth it with wet-and-dry paper if necessary.

6 Paint the unicorn white. Once dry, add detail in pale purple. Varnish and allow to dry. Apply glue to the feet and stand in position centre stage, propping it up with non-hardening modelling clay if required.

Materials and Equipment You Will Need
Pencil • 2mm (⅛in) cardboard • Steel ruler • Scalpel • Gouache paint: purple, yellow and blue • Paintbrushes • Scissors • Furnishing catalogue • Spray adhesive • Acrylic varnish • Strong glue • Modelling polymer clay • Modelling tool (optional) • Wet-and-dry (silicon carbide) paper • Acrylic paint: white and pale purple • Non-hardening modelling clay (optional)

ABSTRACT HAIRSLIDE

Here silver leaf is applied to glow-in-the-dark polymer clay that is then embossed with the spiral patterns of some old earrings to create an intruiging effect. In the dark, a subtle glow emanates from the tiny cracks in the silver leaf. You can use any type of jewellery as the pattern has a distinct relief. If you do not feel confident about building up your own design, just repeatedly press a piece of metal or plastic jewellery into the polymer clay.

1 Roll out some clay 3mm (⅛in) thick. Draw the shape you want on card and cut it out. Place the card on the clay, then cut around it using a scalpel.

2 Carefully apply silver leaf to the clay shape by passing a brayer over it (see Basic Techniques).

3 Create a regular pattern around the edge of the silver-leafed clay by pressing interestingly shaped jewellery or buttons into it to leave indentations.

4 Fill in the central area with a random pattern applied in the same way as in step 3, but using different shapes if you wish.

5 Wearing a dust mask, lightly brush the surface of the hairslide (barrette) around the edge with bronze powder.

6 Slip a small piece of thin card through the full width of the hairslide clip, then place the decorated clay shape on top. The clay will mould itself to the curved shape of the hairslide but the card will prevent it sagging too much. Bake in this position, following the manufacturer's instructions. When cool, varnish and glue the back on to the hairslide clip.

Materials and Equipment You Will Need
½ block glow-in-the-dark polymer clay • Pencil • Thin card (stock) • Scissors • Scalpel • Silver leaf • Brayer • Old jewellery or buttons • Dust mask • Dark blue bronze power • Hairslide (barrette) clip • Varnish • Strong glue

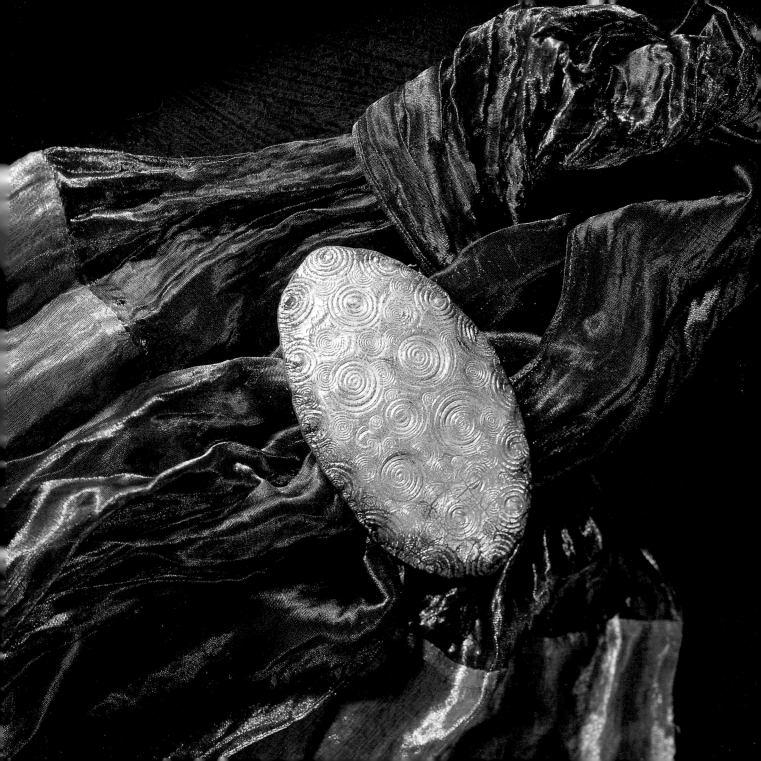

TIGER DOOR PLAQUE

Impish tigers are used here for a child's door plaque, but you can make any design you want with any message. Attach the plaque using heavy-duty self-adhesive tabs. For outdoor use, coat the plaque with at least two thick coats of varnish after making a fixing hole at each corner. Be careful not to turn the screws too tightly when attaching it. The individual tiger's head can be used to make buttons. Make two holes where the nostrils are for the thread before baking.

1 Roll out a rectangle of white clay, about 13cm x 8cm x 5mm (5 x 3 x ¼in), to form the base plate. Make 12 strips 8cm (3in) long and 3mm (⅛in) thick and lay them on the base.

2 For the border, roll out two sausages from black clay, 10cm (½in) in diameter and a little longer than the length of the base of the door plaque. Evenly cut the sausages in half lengthways.

3 Cut the black strips to exactly fit around the sides of the base, mitreing the ends for a neat finish. Arrange them around the edge of the base, smoothing the joints with your fingers.

4 From a 26cm x 7mm x 1mm (10 x ¼ x ¹⁄₁₆in) strip of white clay, cut about 32 triangles. Arrange these at staggered intervals along the border.

5 To make the tigers' faces, roll three balls of white clay and flatten them to form discs 2.5cm (1in) in diameter and 2cm (¾in) thick. Pinch out two ear shapes on each. Place a piece of paper over the shape then smooth using the brayer.

▶

Materials and Equipment You Will Need
2 blocks white polymer clay • Brayer • Scalpel • ½ block black polymer clay • Small amount pink polymer clay • Smoothing tool • Smooth paper

6 Roll a short 3mm (⅛in)-diameter cane from the pink clay and cut into nine slices 1mm (¹⁄₁₆in) thick. Roll each into a ball and flatten into 5mm (¼in)-diameter discs. Place two discs on each face for the cheeks and smooth over. Cut the remaining three discs in half for the ear inserts and press in position.

7 Roll a thin thread of black clay and cut into six thin slices. Roll into balls and flatten for the eyes. Cut short lengths of black thread for the smiling mouths. Press into position using a pin.

8 Cut three triangles and three thin strips from the black clay to make the arrow-shaped noses. Press these into position using a pin.

9 Cut 18 black triangles, long sides 5mm (¼in) and short side 3mm (⅛in). Place three triangles on each side of the faces. Cut nine thinner triangles and arrange between the ears to make fringes.

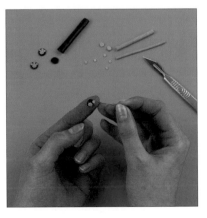

10 Roll a 5mm (¼in)-diameter black cane. Roll two pink canes, one 1mm (¹⁄₁₆in), the other 3mm (⅛in) in diameter. Cut four black discs, four from the thicker pink cane and 12 from the thinner pink cane. Roll the discs into balls and squash flat. Place one large and three small pink discs on each of the black discs to make the paws.

11 Roll a 5mm (¼in)-diameter black cane, carefully slice it in half lengthways to form two even-width strips and use these to form letters. If more letters are required, make the cane narrower and longer so it goes further.

12 Arrange the tiger heads, paws and letters on the plaque and gently press them in place without distorting them. Line a baking tray with greaseproof (waxed) paper and bake following the manufacturer's instructions. Remove the paper from the plaque immediately after baking.

MOBILE JUGGLERS

Mobiles can be structured in an infinite number of ways, and polymer clay is light enough to be made up into interesting shapes to suspend from them. They are fun to make and well suited to a circus theme. Here, four jugglers are modelled in the same basic shape to hang in formation from a frame made out of a bent coathanger. These jugglers have been painted, but you could make them using bright polymer clay colours instead.

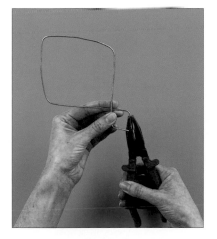

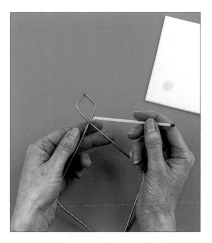

1 Using strong pliers or wire cutters, cut the hook and twisted section off a wire coathanger and discard. Fashion half of the remaining wire into a double diamond shape as illustrated.

2 Spray the shaped wire with gold paint, following the manufacturer's instructions, and leave to dry. Glue the wires together to secure the point where they cross and leave to dry.

3 Mould four thumbnail-sized pieces of clay into egg shapes for the jugglers' heads. Trim an earring wire, form a hook in the end and embed this in one of heads. Repeat for the other heads.

Materials and Equipment You Will Need

Wire coathanger • Pliers or wire cutters • Gold aerosol car paint • Epoxy resin glue • ¼ block modelling polymer clay • Earring wires with loops • Modelling tools • Scalpel or pastry cutters • Dressmaker's needle • Wet-and-dry (silicon carbide) paper (optional) • Acrylic paint: purple, red and yellow • Paintbrush • Varnish • Nylon fishing line • Shell-shaped jewellery findings (optional) • Gold cord or ribbon for hanging

4 Roll a small sausage of clay for the arms and legs, and mould a rounded oblong for the torso. Assemble the parts, shaping the doubled legs into a curve. Using a modelling tool, smooth over the joins.

6 If necessary, smooth any rough edges using wet-and-dry paper.

8 Loop a double thickness of fishing line through the ring on a juggler's head and thread on a bead and a star. Use jewellery findings to keep these in position, or knot the line and glue. Repeat; do not thread a star for the fourth juggler.

5 Roll out some clay and cut out four stars, two a little larger than the others, thick enough to be pierced by a needle. Either cut around a template using a scalpel or use pastry cutters. Roll five marble-sized beads. Pierce through all the pieces with the needle, then bake them with the four jugglers' figures, following the manufacturer's instructions.

7 Paint a purple, red and yellow harlequin pattern on to the figures and leave to dry. Paint the beads red with a yellow pattern and leave to dry. Spray the stars gold. Varnish all these pieces once the paint is dry, and leave to dry again.

9 Tie the jugglers to the wire shape, with the starless one tied to the top corner. Hang the remaining bead inside the small diamond. Dab glue on the knots to prevent the line from slipping. Tie a length of gold cord or ribbon to the top for hanging. Glue the large stars on either side, sandwiching the wire in between.

POLY MERMAID

This delightful mermaid would enjoy basking among a collection of shells on a sandy shelf in a steamy bathroom. Her tail is made of stuffed fabric and is decorated with rows of beads and sequins. The modelling involved for her torso, head and arms is very simple, and translucent clay is used to give her a lovely watery hue. The mermaid's golden tresses are ingeniously made from an unravelled piece of cord, which is glued on to her head.

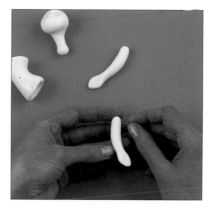

1 Roll a quarter of the clay into a ball and form into the mermaid's head. Draw out the neck to one side, rounding it off into a wider knob. Pinch out the nose and use a needle to make nostrils. Pierce a hole through the side of the neck, halfway down.

2 For the mermaid's midriff, roll a thick, stumpy log. Roll the middle between your index fingers to shape the waist. Make concave recesses in each end with your thumbs. Pierce holes at the front and back of the top and bottom.

3 Fashion two stylized arms and hands from more translucent clay and pierce the top of each with a needle. Bake all of the body parts in the oven, following the manufacturer's instructions.

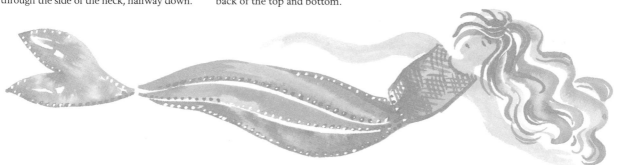

Materials and Equipment You Will Need

1 block translucent polymer clay • Sewing needle and thread • Acrylic paint: blue, red and yellow • Fine paintbrush • Varnish • Thin card (stock) • Pencil • Scissors • 2 different fabrics • Wadding (batting) • Pipe cleaner • Beads • Sequins • Gold cord • Glue

4 Wash the mermaid's face with soap and water to remove any surface grease. Using a fine paintbrush, paint on the features. You can use the image here as a guide or create your own design. Allow to dry.

6 Make a template for the tail shape and cut out the fabric. Cut a bodice from different fabric. With wrong sides together, sew the seams then turn right side out. Gather in the top of the tail fin and sew to the tail. Pad the bodice with wadding and stitch across the top, leaving a gap for the neck.

8 Push a pipe cleaner down inside the tail and stuff with wadding. Decorate the tail by sewing on rows of beads and sequins. Stitch the tail to the mermaid's midriff, sewing through the holes made previously.

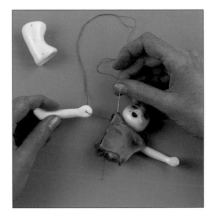

5 Suspend each body part from a thread and dip it into varnish. Hang the pieces up until they are dry.

7 Insert the mermaid's neck and stitch the bodice to the neck. Attach the arms by sewing through the previously made holes to the bodice. Stitch the bodice to the top of the midriff sewing through the previously made holes.

9 Untangle a piece of cord and brush it out to make it look like hair. Glue the hair to the mermaid's head.

MIRROR WITH LIZARDS

Decorated mirror frames are very fashionable, and this one is easy and fun to make. The colourful, bright-eyed lizards would be an ideal decoration for a child's bedroom, or they would add a witty note to your bathroom wall. A cheap mirror with a plastic surround was used here, the surround being broken off with pliers and replaced with polymer clay. The repeat motif is a good, rhythmic way of filling the shape but a single lizard would also be very effective.

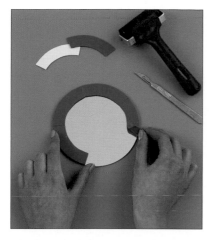

1 Roll out the light turquoise clay to about 5mm (¼in) thick. Cut five curved strips (see the template at the back of the book) and place carefully around the edge of the mirror.

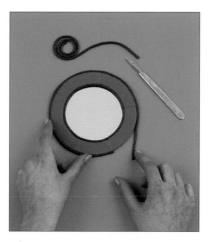

2 From the fluorescent mixed pink and magenta clay roll out two long sausages, one slightly thicker than the other. Use the thinner sausage to edge the inner ring of the border, and the thicker sausage to edge the outer ring.

3 From the dark turquoise clay, fashion 20 lizard legs. Roll short sausages, flatten one end and bend for the knee and foot joints.

4 For each body, roll a tapered sausage from a medium-bead-sized piece of dark turquoise clay. Create a neck in the thicker end by rolling between your two index fingers and flatten out the head shape. Make four more lizard bodies.

►

Materials and Equipment You Will Need
1 block light turquoise polymer clay • Brayer • Scalpel • Round mirror, 13.5cm (5¼in) in diameter • ½ block fluorescent mixed pink and magenta polymer clay (2:1)• 3 blocks dark turquoise polymer clay • Small amount polymer clay: grey, black, and white • Smoothing tool • D-ring • Epoxy resin glue

5 Roll tiny beads from grey, black and white clay for the eyes. Position the grey beads first and gently flatten them, then add the black and finally the white beads on top.

6 Roll thin strands of light turquoise clay to make a stripe for each lizard's back and its legs.

7 Make a thin tapering sausage from the pink clay and slice it thinly using a scalpel to make subtly graded discs. Make about 18 discs per lizard. Roll the discs into balls, flatten and apply to either side of the back stripe.

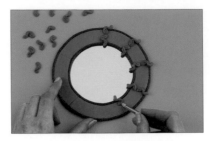

8 Position the legs at equal intervals on the mirror surround so that all the front legs cover up the joins. Press them into position using a smoothing tool.

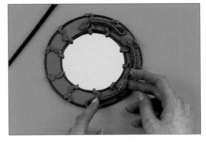

9 Place the lizards' bodies on top of the legs, carefully but firmly enough to ensure that they join properly. Bake the mirror for three-quarters of the manufacturer's recommended baking time.

10 Form another, thicker pink sausage and flatten it into a flat circle using the brayer. Press it in position around the back of the mirror edge, making sure that it adheres well.

11 Roll out a thin sheet of pink clay and trim a semi-circular shape to fit within the back surround. Bake for the remainder of the recommended cooking time.

12 To position the D-ring for hanging, loop a thin strip of clay through the ring and make an indentation on the semi-circular shape but do not attach it yet. Remove the strip and the semi-circle and bake separately on a flat surface. When cool, glue the shape to the back of the mirror then glue the tab, making sure that the D-ring can still move freely.

CHRISTMAS DECORATIONS

Christmas pastry cutters are ideal for making your own decorations – nothing could be easier! Decorate the shapes with a modelling tool and brush on your own pattern with bronze powder. Glue on small rhinestones for extra sparkle, if you like. Instructions are given here for making one decoration but you will probably want to make several, using different Christmas shapes. As well as hanging them on the Christmas tree, you can suspend them from a door knocker or Christmas wreath.

1 Roll out the clay and press out a shape using a pastry cutter.

3 Using a plastic straw, make a hole in the centre top for hanging.

5 Once the shape has cooled, paint on a protective coat of varnish.

2 Draw on markings with a modelling tool and make indentations for the rhinestones with the blunt end of a paintbrush.

4 Brush on differently coloured bronze powders and blend together. Bake following the manufacturer's instructions.

6 Glue rhinestones in the indentations, using a cocktail stick. Thread a hanging ribbon through the hole.

Materials and Equipment You Will Need

Polymer clay • Roller • Christmas pastry cutters • Modelling tool • Paintbrush • Plastic straw • Bronze powder: various colours • Varnish • Rhinestones • Glue • Cocktail stick (toothpick) • Ribbon

MAGNETIC THEATRE

Bring the thrill of the theatre to your own home with this wonderful miniature theatre. Your children's imaginations will supply the rest. The scenery backdrop is reversible to depict night or day. Other characters can be created to suit your own story, but always use the same basic body shape as it is the most stable. The magnets must all be inserted the correct way around in the base of the figures to attract them to their opposite poles in the control sticks.

1 Spray mount the mirror board on to the polyboard. Once the glue is dry, draw the shape of the theatre (see the template at the back of the book) on to the polyboard then cut out using a scalpel and, for the sides, a steel ruler.

2 Glue on star sequins to decorate the domes. Back strips of gold foil with double-sided tape, and draw then cut out a sawtooth pattern from the foil. Peel off the backing from the tape and stick the foil around the arch, towers and parapets.

3 For the reversible backdrop, spray mount each side of a piece of polyboard with different coloured card. Cut out, and the two side struts. Glue gold foil to the strut ends. Assemble the theatre, using the hard card for the base.

Materials and Equipment You Will Need

Spray adhesive • Sheet blue mirror board • Sheet polyboard • Pencil • Scalpel • Steel ruler • Glue • Star sequins, mixed colours • Gold foil • Double-sided tape • Sheet royal blue thin card (stock) • Sheet fluorescent green thin card (stock) • Sheet very hard cardboard (for the floor) • Sheet dark green thin card (stock) • Scissors

For the Players

1 block polymer clay: light and dark brown • Plexiglass • Small magnets • Cocktail sticks (toothpicks) • Small green beads • Glass-headed dressmaker's pin • Spotted polymer clay (see Basic Techniques) or fabric scrap • Modelling tool • Polymer clay: fluorescent orange, fluorescent green and black • Fuse wire • Pen • Bronze powders • Leaf-shaped pastry cutter • 2 x 2cm (³⁄₄in) flower canes (see Basic Techniques) or plain canes • Pencils • Glue

4 To make the figures, mix light and dark brown clay to create the required shade. For the head, roll a small bead. For the body, roll a 3cm (1¼in)-diameter log about 2cm (¾in) long. Press down more firmly on one side as you roll the log, to make a cone shape.

6 Trim a cocktail stick just long enough to connect the head and body. Push it into the top of the cone, pointed end up. Add features to the head, using small glass heads for eyes and a tiny clay bead for the nose. Push the head on to the body.

8 For the arms, roll two thin sausages of brown clay. Flatten one end for hands and mark fingers using a modelling tool.

5 Press a magnet into the base of the cone, leaving it just a bit proud so that it will glide easily.

7 Wrap the body in a sheet of spotted clay, other patterned clay or, after it has been baked, in fabric. Make a fluorescent green beret from a flat pancake of clay with a fluorescent orange pompom.

9 Attach the arms to the sides of the body, pressing them in firmly. Make the other two figures the same way, but make their shapes different.

10 To make the black cat, roll a bead for the head and a dumpy cone for the body, as in step 4. Pinch the bead into the shape of a cat's head and fix it to the body with a trimmed cocktail stick.

12 To make the tree, cut eight pieces of fuse wire about 20cm (8in) long. Double these over and insert a pen or similar object in the loop. Holding the wires about 6cm (2½in) from the cut ends, twist the wire to form the trunk's core.

14 Make bronze-coated variegated leaves (see Burnished Bronze Necklace project) and slot on to the twigs. Brush on purple bronze powder and bake following the manufacturer's instructions.

11 Roll a thin, tapered sausage for the cat's tail. Use two small green beads for the eyes and attach two triangular-shaped pieces of black clay that resemble ears to the head. Attach the tail. Bake all the figures in the oven, following the clay manufacturer's instructions.

13 Roll scrap clay into a cone then push the wire core through the pointed end to embed it in the clay. Roll again to finish the cone's shape. Divide the wires into three. Twist each group into branches, splaying out the ends as twigs. Trim into shape.

15 To make the magnetic operating sticks for the players, bore a hole in the sides of the flower cane discs to take the sharpened end of a pencil. This will distort the disc's shape, so trim it even. Bake the discs, then glue the pencils in position and glue a magnet on to each flower centre.

BURNISHED BRONZE NECKLACE

Polymer clay simplifies the craft of jewellery-making because stones, which would normally have to be set in metal, can simply be pushed into the clay. Metal leaf and powders readily adhere to the slightly sticky surface of unbaked clay to give it a lustrous richness. This necklace is made using a broad range of colours, but you could just use one if you prefer. Glass beads are used to complete the necklace, but you could make your own beads and coat them with metallic powder.

1 Roll out a piece of black clay, about 4mm (³⁄₁₆in) thick, and cut it in half. Dust lines of bronze powders on to the surface of one piece.

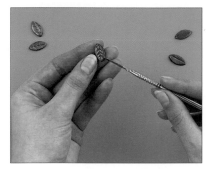

2 Mark vertical lines between the colours, then cut out leaf shapes so that the lines form the central veins. Press in other veining with a modelling tool.

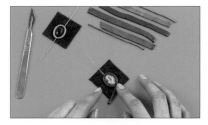

3 Roll the remaining piece of clay slightly thinner and cut it into five or six squares, each 5cm (2in). Place a length of jewellery wire centrally on each square and place a stone on top, slightly off centre to allow room for the leaves. Cut 3mm (⅛in) wide strips from the remaining bronzed clay and wrap these around the stones, cutting off the excess.

4 Arrange three leaves to one side of the stone. The wire should consistently project from the same side of the middle leaf on each square, to allow the necklace to hang in a tight-fitting curve.

5 Press the leaves and stone surround gently but firmly enough to meld them together and to hold the stone securely in place. Cut out around the shape using a scalpel, and smooth along the join at the sides to obliterate it. Bake following the manufacturer's instructions.

6 Carefully varnish the bronzed areas and allow to dry. Using jeweller's pliers, make loops with the wire ends, trimming off excess wire. Hook the pieces together and close up the hooks. Attach the beads at each end of the necklace in the same way and wire on a clasp.

Materials and Equipment You Will Need

1 block black polymer clay • Dust mask • Bronze powders: various colours • Paintbrush • Leaf pastry cutter • Modelling tool • Jewellery wire • Scalpel • Wire cutters • Glass cabochon stones • Varnish • Jeweller's pliers • Bronzed polymer beads or glass beads • Clasp

EYE-CATCHING CUTLERY

Even the most boring cutlery can be given a new lease of life with a set of polymer clay handles. Here, a basic shape is used, but more adventurous shapes can be sculpted. Because cutlery has to stand up to a lot of wear and tear, use the strongest make of polymer clay for the inner layer. For the outside, any of the brands will do. Once baked, polymer clay is waterproof, but it is a good idea to treat the cutlery as if it were bone-handled.

1 For each piece of cutlery, roll out the clay to about 3mm (⅛in) thick and cut into strips. Place two strips around the handle, pressing along the sides to seal.

3 Roll out a sheet of polka dot clay to the width required and wrap around the middle of the handle, positioning the join at the back. Smooth with a smoothing tool.

5 Cut two strips of the second striped clay and wrap around the handle to cover the joins. Join at the back, cutting the ends diagonally to make a good fit.

2 Trim around the handle shape and smooth over the join using your fingers. Cover all the cutlery handles in the same way, then bake them following the manufacturer's instructions.

4 Cut four thin slices of striped clay and wrap these neatly around the top and bottom of the handle. Make the join at the side and try to make it occur on the stripe that is in the darker shade of clay. Smooth over the join using your fingers or a smoothing tool.

6 Using a pin head, make three indentations on each strip, on the front of the handle. Roll three tiny blue balls and press on. Smooth the clay at the top, then wrap with a thin blue strip. Bake following the manufacturer's instructions. Apply a double coat of varnish when cool.

Materials and Equipment You Will Need

2 blocks modelling polymer clay • Brayer • Cutlery • Scalpel • Polka dot polymer clay (see Basic Techniques) • Smoothing tool • Striped polymer clay (see Basic Techniques), in 2 colourways • Tissue blade • Glass-headed dressmaker's pin • Dark blue polymer clay • Matt (flat) varnish

EGYPTIAN BANGLE

It is hard to believe that this exotic-looking piece of jewellery is made from a short length of plastic pipe surrounded by polymer clay. Much of the transformation is brought about by the applied gold leaf and embedded stones. Line the inside of the pipe with a thin layer of the stretched gold clay. To cut the pipe to length, mark a line around and saw through it with a hacksaw. Alternatively, ask the store to cut it to the size you require.

1 Roll out a strip of clay large enough to cover the section of plastic pipe. Apply the gold leaf and crackle the surface using a brayer (see Basic Techniques).

2 Cut the prepared clay exactly to size and wrap it carefully around the pipe, ensuring there are no air bubbles. Try not to touch the surface of the clay much.

3 Join the ends of the clay, taking care not to rub off any gold leaf when smoothing over the join where the ends meet with a smoothing tool.

Materials and Equipment You Will Need
Plastic drainpipe • 1 block black polymer clay • Dutch gold leaf • Brayer • Smoothing tool • Modelling tools • Gemstones • Epoxy resin glue • Acrylic paint: several colours • Fine paintbrush

4 Using a modelling tool, faintly mark a line around the circumference 1cm (½in) from one edge. Measure the circumference, divide the figure by the number of stones you wish to use and mark spacings along the line. Press the gemstones into the clay.

5 Draw a line around each stone, then press an arch around it using a paintbrush.

6 Draw a line around the bangle along the top of the arches.

7 Etch a narrow arch between adjacent arches all around the edge of bangle. This will form the central petal of the stylized Egyptian flower.

8 Draw a pointed petal on either side of the central ones, then add smaller ones in between.

9 Carefully remove the stones from their positions on the bangle and bake the bangle following the manufacturer's instructions. When cool, glue the stones back in place.

10 Paint the flowers and background sections of the bangle in colours of your choice. Leave to dry.

COMPOSITE BEADS

Once you have mastered the art of millefiori (see Basic Techniques), you will be able to use it in a number of exciting ways. Here, slices from a picture cane, combined with a flower cane and a colourful jelly roll, are applied to partially baked polymer clay beads. When fully baked, these wonderfully decorative beads can be strung together to make necklaces. Remember to make holes in the unbaked beads.

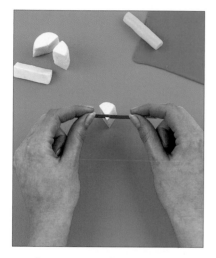

1 Roll a 3cm (1¼in)-diameter log of white clay. Cut it into five wedges from the centre and slice off the sharp angle of each wedge. Roll out a 6cm (2½in) yellow cane and a flat sheet of green clay.

2 Arrange the white triangular wedges, separated by 3mm (⅛in) slivers of green, around the central yellow cane to form a flower. Roll, using a sheet of plexiglass to smooth.

3 Make a jelly roll with 4 x 10cm (1½ x 4in) strips of yellow and fluorescent orange clay (see Basic Techniques). Wrap it in a thin sheet of pale blue clay, about 1mm (¹⁄₁₆in) thick.

Materials and Equipment You Will Need
1 block white polymer clay • Scalpel • Tissue blade • ¼ block yellow polymer clay • 1 block green polymer clay • Plexiglass • ½ block fluorescent orange polymer clay • ¼ block pale blue polymer clay • 6cm (2½in) of 3cm (1in)-diameter picture cane (see Basic Techniques) • 20cm (8in) flower cane • ½ block coral polymer clay • Various-shaped polymer clay beads (see Basic Techniques)

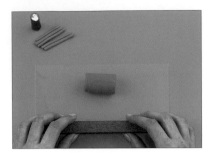

4 Reduce the picture cane to 1cm (½in) in diameter and the flower cane and jelly roll to 5cm (¼in) (see Basic Techniques). Reserve the trimmings for making beads. Cut the jelly roll into 8cm (3in) lengths. Cut an 8cm (3in) length from the duck cane and set the surplus aside.

5 Cut the flower cane into four lengths of 8cm (3in). Arrange them in a cross pattern around the picture cane, interspersed with four jelly roll canes.

6 Roll the assembled canes carefully between your hands to meld them together, then wrap in a 3mm (⅛in) thick sheet of green clay.

7 Cut the cane in half using a tissue blade and rocking while you cut, to avoid distorting the picture. Wrap one of the halves in a 3mm (⅛in) thick sheet of coral clay, cut off the surplus and roll under plexiglass to smooth the sides.

8 Make up several compilation canes, then reduce them further to different sizes. Shave off thin slices to cover the surface of previously prepared disc beads and roll them smooth. It is a good idea to make the canes and the beads compatible sizes.

9 Use some of the surplus picture and flower cane to make borders or sides for the beads. Press them on firmly so they will adhere, and smooth over.

10 Cover previously prepared round beads, filling any triangular-shaped gaps with slices of the surplus small flower or picture cane. If you cover any of the bead holes, simply pierce through them again after you have rolled the surface smooth. Bake all the beads following the manufacturer's instructions.

GLOW-IN-THE-DARK CLOCK

Because it is made with glow-in-the-dark polymer clay, you will be able to read the time from this amusing clock in the dark. The flower and egg motifs are detachable, allowing for other ornaments, such as a candle for a birthday celebration (as long as the candle does not burn right down to the clay), to be attached to the clock in their place. The clock mechanism is inexpensive to buy and is easily assembled.

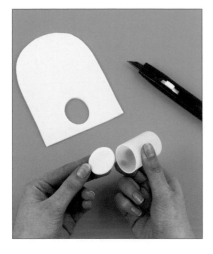

3 Fix the cup over the hole in the clock face and smooth over the join. Mark the hour positions on the circular template and position it on the back plate. Prick through the centre to mark the clock face. Using a narrow tube, stamp out a hole large enough to take the clock spindle.

1 Roll out the glow-in-the-dark clay and trim to a 10 x 13cm (4 x 5in) rectangle 4mm (³⁄₁₆in) thick. Cut a circular template, place at one end and cut around to shape the top. Squeezing an empty plastic pot of a suitable size, stamp out an oval near the bottom.

2 Make templates for a slightly curved strip and for the oval cut out in step 1. Roll out a small quantity of yellow clay and cut out these shapes. Wrap the strip around the oval to form a tapered cup.

4 Roll and cut out two strips of glow-in-the-dark clay 3cm (1¼in) wide by 4mm (³⁄₁₆in) thick. Make one 31cm (12¼in) and the other 10cm (4in) in length. Using a very narrow tube, stamp out a small hole at the mid-point of the longer strip.

Materials and Equipment You Will Need

2³⁄₄ blocks glow-in-the-dark polymer clay • Craft (utility) knife or scalpel • Metal ruler • Thin card (stock) • Pencil • Small flexible plastic pot • ¼ block polymer clay: yellow, light blue, dark blue, light and dark green • Smoothing tool • Dressmaker's pin • Narrow tubes • Jewellery wire • Aluminium foil • Crosshead screw • Ballpoint pen • Jewellery head pins • Epoxy resin glue • Wire cutters • Clock mechanism

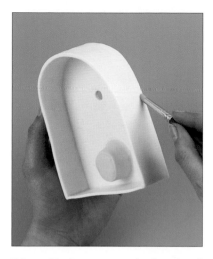

5 Assemble the strips to make the sides of the clock face, smoothing over the joins with a smoothing tool. Fix the sides to the back of the clock face and smooth over the joins using a smoothing tool.

6 Roll a marble-sized piece of light blue clay into an egg shape. Crumble some dark blue clay and roll the egg in this to speckle the surface, without distorting the egg shape.

7 Push two wires, about 1.5cm (⅝in), into the egg. They should project enough to push into the recess to hold the egg in place. Remove the egg and bake it following the manufacturer's instructions.

8 Cut a glow-in-the-dark clay rectangle to cover the bottom section of the back of the clock face. Pack out the cavity with scrunched-up aluminium foil. Bake following the manufacturer's instructions.

9 Twist together thin strips of yellow and light and dark green clay to create a marbled sausage.

10 Cut the sausage into one long and four short pieces. Assemble the pieces to make a central stem with four branches. Taper one end of the stem.

11 Make incisions along the branches and stem and insert wires long enough to protrude from the ends of the branches and the non-tapered end of the stem. Close up the slits and smooth over.

12 Roll out a small piece of yellow clay and form a three-petalled flower. Roll out a small piece of green clay and shape four leaves. Press patterns on these and the flower using the tip of a screw and a pen.

13 Push the flower and leaves on to the wires of the stem and branches and bake following the manufacturer's instructions. When assembled, the tapered stem slots into the hole at the top of the clock.

14 Twist together thin strips of light and dark blue clay and slice off 12 discs. Roll these into balls and flatten. Stamp each with the end of a screw and make a hole in the middle. Bake the discs following the manufacturer's instructions.

15 Push a jewellery head pin through each disc, dab a spot of glue on the back and push the pin into the clock face at an hour marking. When the glue has dried, snip off the excess wire at the back. Hold the clock movement at the back of the clock face. Push the spindle through the hole from the front and screw together.

PICTURE FRAME

The recipe for this project will make a batch of eight to ten frames. The colours are built up in blocks, from which you take slices for each frame. To make a single frame, cut out all the basic shapes from 2mm ($^1/_{16}$in) thick sheets of green clay and cut out all the decoration from blue and black sheets. Lay them on top of one another and roll over them to ensure they adhere. Assemble the frame using pieces of black clay on the back. Make the holes and embroider as described.

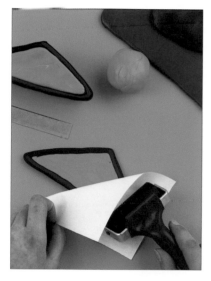

1 Thoroughly mix and blend the green and turquoise clays. Mould a block of the resulting colour into a triangular wedge. Cover with a thin skin of black clay, then cover two sides with a thick blue layer and one side with black. Surround the whole with a thin layer of black. Using the tissue blade, take off a thin 3mm ($^1/_8$in) slice across the wedge (see Basic Techniques). Place a sheet of smooth paper over this and roll the slice smooth. This will be the roof.

2 Make a long oblong block in green clay, measuring about 16 x 2.5 x 3cm (6½ x 1 x 1¼in). Surround it with a thin skin of black clay. Place a thick blue strip along the bottom. Cover the top with black two-thirds of the length and with blue the remainder, and finally with a thin layer of black. Make two smaller oblongs, about 6 x 2 x 3cm (2½ x ¾ x 1¼in), one of black, the other of green. Slice both in half then cut diagonally across each to make triangles.

3 Place a green triangle centrally on top of the oblong block. Add another on either side of the central triangle side. Cut the remaining triangle in half and place at each end. Encircle the entire structure with a thin strip of black clay. Cover one side and halfway along the ridges with a thick blue layer. Cover the other side and the remaining ridges with a thick black layer, then continue with a thin black layer over the blue right down the opposite side.

Materials and Equipment You Will Need

1 block green polymer clay • 1 block turquoise polymer clay • Large block black polymer clay • 2 blocks blue polymer clay • Smooth paper • Brayer • Tissue blade • Scalpel • Needle • Embroidery thread (floss): blue and yellow • Corrugated or thick cardboard • Knitting needle • Jewellery head pin • Jeweller's pliers

4 Invert the black triangles between the green ones and compress the whole assembly, without disorting any of it, to pack all the elements together. Using the tissue blade, take off a 3mm (⅛in) slice. Place a sheet of paper over this and roll smooth. Cut out the black triangle, leaving a black edging. This will be the base.

5 Make up another block, like the base block in step 2, but 16 x 4 x 3cm (6½ x 1½ x 1¼in). Using the tissue blade, take off two thin 3mm (⅛in) slices the length of the oblong. Place a sheet of smooth paper over each and roll them smooth. These will be the sides.

6 Decorate the roof and sides. Make an oval cane of blue wrapped in black and cut three slices for the roof. Make long, thin blue and black sausages to make scroll patterns on the roof and sides. Cut tiny discs from the sausages to make spots.

7 Assemble the frame, securing the elements with small pieces of black clay pressed across the joins at the back.

8 Referring to the finished illustration for guidance, use a needle to make stitching holes. Add more spots to balance the design if you like. Cover the back with a thin layer of black clay, cutting out the window. Place the frame, face up, on a sheet of greaseproof (waxed) paper and bake following the manufacturer's instructions.

9 Stitch through the prepared holes with embroidery threads, referring to the finished illustration.

10 Roll out a 3mm (⅛in) thick black rectangle, slightly larger than the window. Place it over a sheet of corrugated cardboard or other thick cardboard and press all around it to create a pocket. Pierce a hole near the top using a knitting needle and reinforce the hole with a ring of clay.

11 Make a small black-wrapped blue cane, press it into an egg shape and cut six slices. Sandwich a jewellery head pin between a pair of slices and kink the wire with pliers. Repeat with the other slices. Bake these with the pocket, following the manufacturer's instructions.

12 Glue the pocket into position on the front of the frame, pressing along the seams to ensure a good join. The gap should be wide enough to slide in a piece of glass and a picture.

CACTUS CANDELABRA

The cactus shape makes a dramatic, sculptural candelabra and the fluorescent colour ensures it will be a focal point in any room. A basic structure made from wire and aluminium foil is covered with a skin of clay to make the candelabra an economic proposition. Check that the dimensions of the candelabra will fit in your oven before starting work. It will bake more quickly at the top of the oven than at the bottom, so you may need to rotate the candelabra during baking.

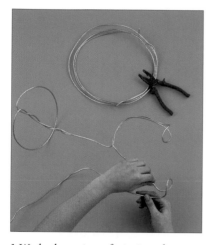

1 Work a long piece of wire into the basic structure of the candelabra. Make a circular base, bend the wire back to the centre then up to make the central stem. Form the three branches, looping the end of each in to make candle-holders. Twist the remaining end in.

2 Spread out five large sheets of foil, one on top of the other. Cut a piece of cardboard the size of a small plate and place it centrally on the foil. Stand the candelabra frame on the card.

3 Fold up the foil, shaping it into a funnel around the wire frame.

4 Pour a jugful or pitcherful of sand into the funnel to pack it out and also to weight the base of the candelabra.

5 Squeeze the foil together around the frame. Fold sheets of foil into thick strips and wrap these around the stem to make a bulbous shape.

Materials and Equipment You Will Need

Malleable wire, about 1.5m (5ft) • Pliers • Aluminium foil • Cardboard • Plate • Scissors • Jug or pitcher • Sand • Wide masking tape • 2 blocks modelling polymer clay • Rolling pin • Scalpel • 2 blocks fluorescent green polymer clay • Polymer clay: fluorescent pink, orange and dark green • Dressmaker's pin • Strong glue

6 Roll the foil strips into cups and tuck them over the wire loops. Bind the cups in place to the required thickness using more folded foil.

7 Wrap masking tape around the structure to completely cover it.

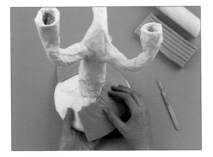

8 Roll the clay into broad strips, about 3mm (⅛in) thick, and cover the candelabra with them. Do not press too hard as this will spoil its smooth form. Smooth over the joins.

9 Tuck the ends of the clay over the candle-holder edges. Bake for 10 minutes.

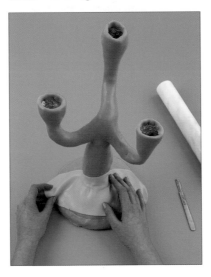

10 Roll out the fluorescent green clay into thin sheets and use it to completely cover the baked modelling clay, smoothing over the joins. Bake the candelabra for another 10 minutes.

11 Roll one thick and one thin fluorescent green sausage, one thick fluorescent pink sausage and one thinner fluorescent orange sausage. Cut thin discs from all of these, make into balls then flatten. Place pink dots on the larger green discs and orange dots on the smaller green discs. Pierce through both layers with a pin to help them hold together. Place the dots on a flat tray and bake following the manufacturer's instructions.

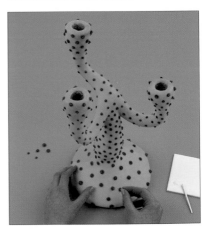

12 Glue the cooked dots to the candelabra to transform it into a 'cactus'.

FUNKY FURNITURE

Give a new lease of life to a doll's house with this miniscule set of fluorescent furniture. The clay is first made up into a striped block, a double-layered sandwich slab and a jelly roll. These are then cut into slices to make the furniture. The quantities of clay quoted are enough to make one polka dot armchair, a table and a set of four dining chairs. Adjust the size of the furniture if necessary to suit the dimensions of your own doll's house.

1 For the armchair, prepare the following from fluorescent orange and yellow clay: a 4 x 6 x 2.5cm (1½ x 2½ x 1in) striped block; a double-layered sandwich slab, about 4cm x 7cm x 5mm (1½ x 2¾ x ¼in); and a 6cm (2½in) length of 2cm (¾in)-diameter jelly roll (see Basic Techniques).

2 Cut out the armchair back from the double-layered slab using a scalpel. The base should be 5cm (2in) wide. From top to base it should be 6cm (2½in) and its broadest width should be 7cm (2¾in).

3 Cut three thin slices from the jelly roll and set aside. Cut the remainder in half. Holding a tissue blade at an angle, slice a wedge off each end of the striped block to make it trapezium-shaped.

4 Assemble the armchair. Place the back on top of the trapezium, longest length up, pressing firmly to secure it, then smooth over the joins. Place the halved jelly roll pieces on either side of the seat for arms and press the back into them. Then puff it out in the centre by pressing with your fingers through the back.

Materials and Equipment You Will Need

1 block fluorescent orange polymer clay • 1 block fluorescent yellow polymer clay • Ruler • Scalpel • Tissue blade • Smoothing tool • Glass-headed dressmaker's pin • 1 block fluorescent light turquoise polymer clay • 1 block fluorescent green polymer clay • Flat wooden cocktail sticks (toothpicks) • Plexiglass • Standard cocktail sticks (toothpicks) • Wire-cutters • Epoxy resin glue • Pair of dividers

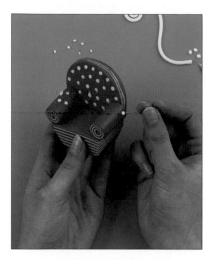

5 Make a thin sausage of fluorescent yellow clay, slice it into discs and roll into tiny balls. Apply the balls to the armchair to create a polka dot pattern, using a glass-headed pin (see Basic Techniques).

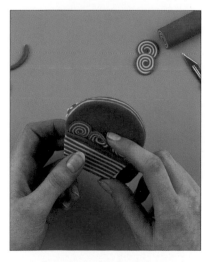

6 Reinforce the back behind the armchair by running a length of flattened fluorescent orange sausage along the join, then place the thin jelly roll slices along the ridge.

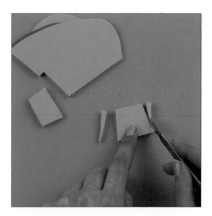

7 For the table and chairs, prepare a sandwich slab about 12cm x 8cm x 6mm (4¾ x 3 x ¼in) (see Basic Techniques), using light turquoise and fluorescent green clay. For each chair, cut trapezium-shaped seats with the longest side 3.5cm (1½in), its parallel 2.5cm (1in) and the two sides 3cm (1¼in). Cut trapezium-shaped backs with the same length parallels but sides of 2cm (¾in). Smooth around the edges.

8 Push the wedge ends of three toothpicks into the bottom edge of each chair back, leaving 2.5cm (1in) protruding.

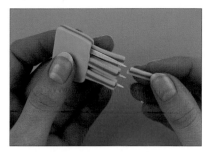

9 Cut six thin 2cm (¾in) strips from the sandwich slab for each chair. Sandwich the toothpicks between these, leaving the points uncovered. Press between finger and thumb to join up at the sides.

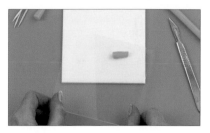

10 Roll an 8cm (3in)-long, 5mm (¼in)-diameter green clay log for each chair. Cut each one into four chair legs and taper the shape by rolling and pressing one end. Insert a cocktail stick into the narrower end of each leg. Bake the legs standing up, and the backs lying down, following the manufacturer's instructions.

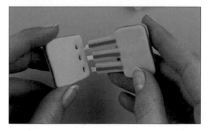

11 Press the baked backs into the unbaked seats to make holes.

▶

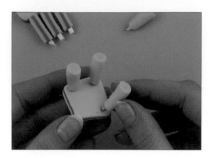

12 Trim the cocktail sticks in the legs, leaving just enough to embed in the seat. Press the legs into the undersides of the seats. Remove the legs and bake the seats.

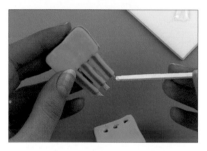

13 Assemble the chairs. Glue the legs in position. Once dry, glue on to the chair backs. Support until the glue is dry.

14 Make another sandwich slab measuring a minimum of 9cm (3½in) square. Using a pair of dividers, lightly mark a 9cm (3½in) circle. Mark a cross at the centre and mark 2cm (¾in) along each line from the centre point. Cut out the circle and smooth around the edge.

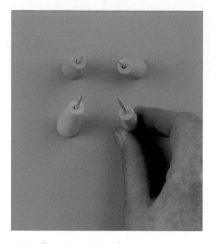

15 Roll a 14cm (5½in)-long, 1.5cm (⅝in)-diameter green clay log. Cut into four table legs. Taper them and insert cocktail sticks as described in step 10. Bake them standing up and leaning slightly inwards.

16 Trim the cocktail sticks, leaving just enough to embed in the tabletop. Press them into the tabletop to mark their positon, remove them and place the tabletop on a piece of greaseproof paper the right way up. Bake following the manufacturer's instructions. When cool, glue in the legs.

TINY TEA SET

This Lilliputian tea set would make a delightful present for any child or doll's house enthusiast. Polymer clay is ideally suited to small-scale working as its elasticity allows fine shapes and details to be modelled. The colours remain separate even when the clay is squashed into a small form. Spots are a cheerful decoration and easy to paint on to such miniature items. You may prefer to use a colour and pattern to match an existing doll's house decor.

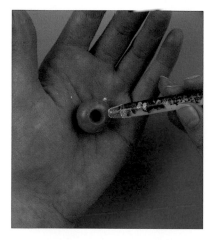

3 Press the spout on to the pot and stroke the end into a curve.

1 Roll a marble-sized piece of clay into a ball with your hands. Dip the end of a pen, or similar object, into the flour and push it into the ball with a screwing action to create a pot shape.

2 For the spout, roll a sausage shape and cut off a small amount. Roll this between your little fingers to taper the shape. Cut a small 'V' out of one end.

4 Roll another, thinner, sausage and cut off enough for a handle. Fix the top of the handle by pressing the head of a pin on the underside, then loop the sausage over and fix the bottom.

Materials and Equipment You Will Need
½ block polymer clay • 5ml/1 tsp flour or talcum powder • Pen or similar object • Scalpel • Glass-headed dressmaker's pin • Small marble • Washers: 2cm (¾in) and 1.5cm (⅝in) • Palette knife or spatula • Small can white enamel paint • Paintbrush • Varnish

5 Roll three small balls, one pea-sized, one a little larger and one a little smaller. Squash the largest ball against a marble to shape it into a curved disc for the lid.

6 Press the smallest ball on to the lid to make a knob. Squash the pea-sized ball into a disc that will just fit inside the rim of the teapot, then press it centrally to the underside of the lid.

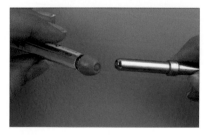

7 To make the teacups, roll a pencil-thin sausage, and slice it into four lengths measuring about 5mm (¼in). Push the end of a pen, dipped in flour or talcum powder, into the end of each length to hollow it out. Before removing the pen, indent the other end of each cup so that they will stand up better.

8 Make each cup handle from a thin thread of clay, attaching it in the same way as for the teapot (see step 4).

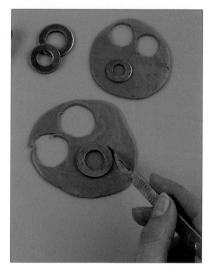

9 For the saucers and plates, use the washers as templates. Roll out a piece of clay about 3mm (⅛in) thick and cut around each washer four times.

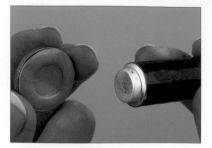

10 Hold the larger washer against each plate and push the end of a pen or similar object through the hole to make an impression for the inner circle.

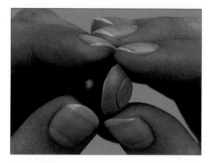

11 Press the smaller washer against each saucer to make an indentation, then curve it around the marble. Bake all the pieces in the oven following the manufacturer's instructions and allow to cool.

12 Decorate with tiny spots of white paint. Allow to dry then varnish as required.

SHIMMERING EARRINGS

Being lighter than metal, polymer clay allows large, bold designs to be worn as earrings, especially when fitted as here with cushioned clips. The tiers of these glamorous earrings swing as the wearer moves, glittering as they catch the light. For a less flamboyant version, make the earrings using only one of the tiers. Gold leaf scrolls, different-shaped gemstones and droplet beads all contribute to the effect, and the earrings are richly marked with decorative indentations and lines.

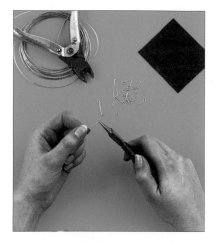

1 Cut 12 lengths of wire 2cm (¾in) long and form a loop in one end of each. Cut two lengths of 3cm (1¼in) and two of 6cm (2½in) and form loops at both ends of each. Cut a sheet of black clay into squares to make backing sheets: two x 3cm (1¼in) squares for the top tiers; two x 4 x 3cm (1½ x 1¼in) for the central tiers; and two x 1.5cm (⅝in) squares for the bottom tiers.

2 Lay three short wires along the bottom of each middle-sized backing sheet and press them in with the brayer. Lay a long wire down the centre of each large backing sheet with a short, single-hooked wire on either side and press in. Lay the remaining short, single-hooped wires one on each of the small backing sheets and press in.

3 Press an oval stone on to each of the middle-sized backing sheets. Cut two strips, 3mm (⅛in) wide, from the gold-leafed clay and wrap securely around each stone, trimming off any excess. Add more strips to decorate.

4 Cut two lengths, 3cm (1¼in), from the gold-leafed slab and pinch both ends to taper them. Shape into scrolls and press in position on the middle-sized backing sheets to cover the wires, pushing the wires in a bit more if necessary. Cut two small squares of gold-leafed clay, cut in half diagonally and place above the scrolls. Press decorative indentations and lines with the head and shank of a pin around the border. Trim off the excess backing sheet.

▶

Materials and Equipment You Will Need

Jeweller's wire • Wire cutters • Round-nosed (snub-nosed) jeweller's pliers • ¼ block black polymer clay • Brayer • ¼ block black polymer clay with gold leaf applied (see Basic Techniques) • Gemstones: oval 1cm (½in) long; rectangular 1.5cm (⅝in) long; round 5mm (¼in) diameter • Scalpel • Dutch gold leaf • Dressmaker's pins • Palette knife or spatula • Eyelet or similarly shaped object • Smoothing tool • Varnish • Paintbrush • Large clip-on earring backs • Epoxy resin glue • 10 droplet beads

7 Make six tiny beads, roll them in gold leaf and use them to decorate the tops of the middle tiers. Trim off the excess backing sheet.

10 Varnish all the gold leaf surfaces and allow to dry. Glue the clip-on earring backs to the backs of the first tier.

5 Press the square stones centrally on to the two large backing sheets. Cut a 1.5cm (⅝in) square and a 1cm (½in) square from the gold-leafed clay. Cut both of these in half diagonally to create four triangles. Press a larger triangle above each stone and a smaller one beneath. Cut four thin strips of gold-leafed clay to fit on each side of the stones.

8 Place one of the remaining stones on each of the small backing squares. Cut two strips of gold-leafed clay 3cm (1¼in) long and wrap them around the stones. Trim off the excess backing sheet.

11 Join the tiers together, using jeweller's pliers to close up the hooks.

6 Using a palette knife or spatula, press in all the pieces to secure a tight fit around the stones. Take care not to distort the shapes. Cut two thin strips 4.5cm (1¾in) long from the gold-leafed clay, curl them into scrolls and place one under each bottom triangle. Use an eyelet to stamp a circular marking on the top triangles.

9 Using a smoothing tool or your finger, go around the edges of each piece to make sure all the surfaces are melded together. Bake following the manufacturer's instructions and allow to cool.

12 Hang droplet beads from the free hooks, closing up the hooks. The bottom ones can be slightly bigger than the others.

STARBURST HAND MIRROR

"Mirror, mirror on the wall, who is the fairest of them all?" Although this mirror is not fixed to the wall, it is certainly reminiscent of fairy tales and mythology. The magical effect is achieved by encasing the mirror between two layers of polymer clay which have been covered with stretched copper leaf; copper leaf changes colour when heated, enhancing its appearance. The surround is embellished with glass gemstones and painted. The handle is reinforced with wire.

1 Roll out a 5mm (¼in)-thick sheet of clay, about 3cm (1½in) larger all around than the mirror. Apply copper leaf and crackle the surface (see Basic Techniques). Press the mirror into the centre of the clay to embed it firmly.

3 Prepare a thin strip of clay with copper leaf, rolled a little more thinly to give a finer crackle. Press it on to the clay base to surround the mirror.

5 Using a modelling tool, press all around the inner and outer edges of the mirror surround to neaten them and to secure the mirror in position. Do the same around the cross points.

2 Cut two pieces of rectangular clay to form the handle. Press one into the edge of the mirror base. Prepare the second piece with crackled copper leaf as in step 1 and set it aside for use in step 8.

4 Cut out three trapezium-shaped pieces of clay to form the three points of the cross. Apply copper leaf and crackle the surface as in step 3, then press the points in place.

6 Place a small cabochon stone on the mirror surround opposite each cross point and the handle. Score the cross points outwards to create a ray-like pattern.

Materials and Equipment You Will Need
Large block black polymer clay • Copper leaf • Mirror • Scalpel • Modelling tool • 4 small blue glass cabochon stones • Wire •
3 large gemstones • Acrylic paint: mauve, coral, blue and white • Paintbrush

7 Etch a double-tiered zigzag pattern radiating out from the mirror surround to give a sunburst effect.

8 Bend a piece of wire to form a hook at one end. Embed it along the length of the handle with the hook towards the mirror. Cover with the second part of the handle prepared in step 2, pressing the edges together well.

9 Carefully mould the zigzag sunburst pattern around the mirror surround to create a staggered ray effect as shown in the photograph. Cut off the excess clay using a scalpel.

10 Press the large gemstones along the handle as shown and carefully delineate the area around each of them using the modelling tool.

11 Roll out a thin piece of clay and apply copper leaf to it. Cut it into three narrow strips and surround each gemstone with one. Press a pattern into the strips to secure the stones in position. Bake following the manufacturer's instructions.

12 Highlight the details with differently coloured paints: variegated mauve on the outer spikes; variegated coral on the inner spikes; variegated blue on the cross points and down the handle (see Ornamental Book Cover project, steps 10 and 11).

ORNAMENTAL BOOK COVER

A handsome plaque glued to the front of a clothbound book or diary, or to the lid of a box, will make it into something special. This one is made from a silver-leafed slab of polymer clay which has been moulded and painted. Silver and gold leaf give an opulent feel, but a cheaper option would be to paint the slab with metallic paint after the clay has been baked. If you wish to devise your own design, transfer it to the clay by pricking through a piece of paper with a pin.

1 Cut off a quarter of the clay block and roll ir into a ball.

3 Press a similarly sized, clean-edged circular object, such as a length of tubing, over the dome to give it a regular shape.

5 Roll out a rough rectangle, about 8cm x 11cm x 5mm (3 x 4 ½ x ¼in). Apply silver leaf to the surface and give it a fine crackle (see Basic Techniques). Lightly mark a cross to locate the centre and press the dome shape into the clay. Cut out a true rectangle using a ruler and scalpel.

2 Squash the ball into a flat-bottomed dome shape.

4 Dab silver leaf on to the dome to make irregular map-like shapes, suggestive of a globe of the world.

Materials and Equipment You Will Need

Large block black polymer clay • Scalpel • Clean-edged circular object • Silver leaf • Rolling pin • Metal ruler • Modelling tools • 4 blue glass cabochon stones • Acrylic paint: turquoise, purple, blue, red and white • Paintbrushes: fine and medium • Varnish • Epoxy resin glue

►

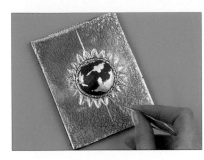

6 Delineate around the globe and score radial zigzag lines around it using a modelling tool or bent wire.

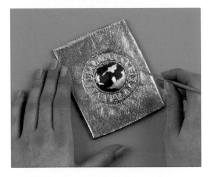

7 Encircle the zigzag pattern with two parallel circles and sculpt them in.

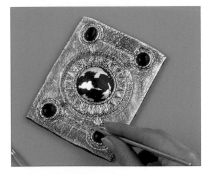

8 Place a blue cabochon stone in each corner. Encircle them with patterning as around the globe, connecting them at top and bottom with horizontal lines.

9 Roll out a thin sheet of clay, apply silver leaf to it then cut it into strips. Cut each strip into a zigzag to make tiny triangles. Press these around each stone as decoration and to hold it firmly in place.

10 Paint on the base colours, leaving black edging around the 'continents' on the globe. When dry, add white to all the colours except turquoise and paint thickish stripes all over the base.

11 Adding yet more white to the basic colours, paint on finer lines to create a variegated appearance.

12 Varnish the surface, taking care not to put varnish on the stones, and allow to dry. Glue on to a book or box.

TEMPLATES

If the templates need to be enlarged, use a grid system or a photocopier or scanner. For the grid system, trace the template and draw a grid of evenly spaced squares over your tracing. To scale up, draw a large grid on to another piece of paper. Copy the outline on to the larger square, taking each square individually and drawing the relevant part of the outline in the larger square. Finally, draw over the lines to make sure they are continuous. Alternatively, two different sizes of graph paper may be used.

MAGNETIC THEATRE PP54–7

LIZARD MIRROR PP49–51

THREE-DIMENSIONAL PICTURE PP36–7

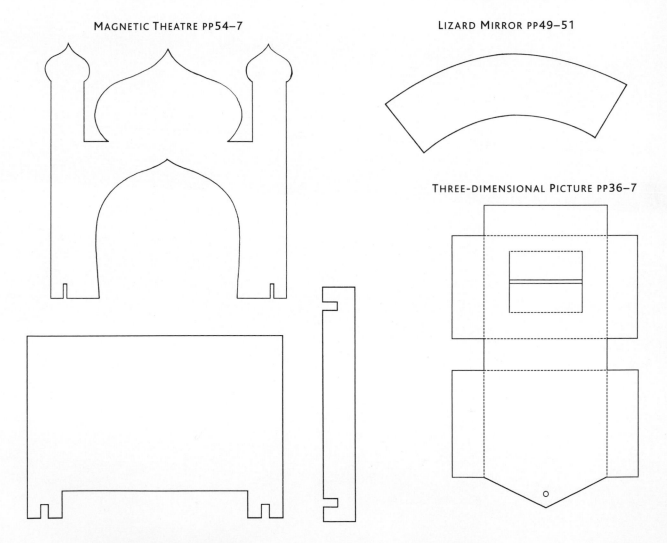

MERMAID PP46–8

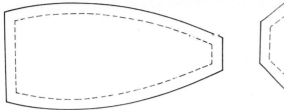 

SUPPLIERS

Listed here are a few major stores, and some of the suppliers used by the author.

United Kingdom
Alec Tiranti Ltd
70 High Street
Theale RG7 5AR
Tel: 0845 123 2100
www.tiranti.co.uk
Sculpey, modelling tools, gold and silver leaf and bronze powders

Swann Morton Ltd
Owlerton Green
Sheffield S6 2BJ
Tel: 0114 234 4231
www.swann-morton.com
Craft (utility) knives and scalpels, including skin graft blades

Craftmill
Tel: 0161 484 5888
www.polymer-clay.co.uk
Suppliers of polymer clay, tools and accessories

ClayAround
Tel: 0168 664 0745
www.clayaround.com
Suppliers of polymer clay, tools and accessories

Craftcellar
Tel: 0113 815 0050
www.craftcellar.co.uk
Suppliers of polymer clay, tools and accessories

H S Walsh & Sons
44 Hatton Garden
London EC1N 8ER
Tel: 020 7242 3711
www.hswalsh.com
Clock mechanisms

USA
Polymer Clay Express
Tel: 301-882-7260
www.polymerclayexpress.com
International supplier of polymer clay, tools and accessories

Polymer Clay Superstore
Tel: 610-693-4039
www.polymerclaysuperstore.com
Suppliers of polymer clay, tools and accessories

The Polymer Arts
www.thepolymerarts.com/SuppliesTPA_01.pdf
Resource list of suppliers of polymer clay and accessories

Jo-ann Fabric and Craft Stores
www.joann.com/crafts/general-crafts/clay/
Fabric and craft supplier

AliExpress
www.aliexpress.com
Wholesale polymer clay supplier

Canada
Opus
1360 Johnston Street
Granville Island
Vancouver V6H 3S1
Tel: 604-736-7028
www.opusartsupplies.com
Art supplies

The Pottery Supply House
1120 Speers Road
Oakville, ON
L6L 2X4
Tel: 905-849-5540
www.pshcanada.com
Clays and modelling tools

Bead Works
2154 Queen St E
Toronto, ON
Tel: 416-693-0780
www.beadworksjo.com
Beads and beading supplies

Lee Valley
1275 Morningside Ave
Toronto, ON
M1B 3W1
Tel: 416 746 0850
www.leevalley.com
Punches, craft knives, pliers, scalpels, dividers, wire cutters

Shades of Clay
428 Sherin Drive
Oakville, ON
L6L 4J5
Tel: 416-452-5204
www.shadesofclay.com
Arts and crafts supplier specializing in clay

Australia
Over The Rainbow
www.polymerclay.com.au
Beads, jewellery, resin and polymer clay supplies

The Whimsical Bead
www.thewhimsicalbead.com.au
Polymer clay, tools and accessories

Clay Princess
www.clayprincess.com.au
Specialist supplier of polymer clay, along with general crafts

INDEX